24 Week Marathon Training Schedu

- ➢ **Plan notes**

  The plan is broken down into two training schedules.

- ➢ **Schedule 1**

  This is an eight-week 'lead-in' schedule that will prepare you for the main training plan. Schedule 1 culminates in a 10K event, which is an ideal target for you to focus on.

- ➢ **Schedule 2**

  This is the main 16-week training schedule that will take you through to race day. For each session in the plan, follow the protocols for warm-up, mobility, main session, cool-down and flexibility outlined earlier. Completely new exercisers should start at week one but if you have been doing some training, you can jump in at a later week. Simply check the week-by-week chart to see which week best matches your current activity levels and then start at that point.

  There is flexibility within the plan for switching training sessions around during the week to fit in with your other commitments such as work, home, family etc. The key point is to ensure that your training is balanced each week, including flexibility, CV and rest.

> **Supper tip**
>
> Don't be a slave to the programme! The training plan is designed with rest days, recovery sessions and lower volume weeks. This will ensure your body has time to adapt to the training. However, every runner is different and if you feel that an extra days rest will be beneficial to your training, simply take out one of the shorter sessions in that week.

If you find it difficult to complete some weeks due to lack of training time, always try to complete the long run sessions. The most important factor with training for the marathon is to build endurance so try to complete all the long runs.

Training Plans

Schedule 1: Building up to the main marathon schedule

Week 1 First Steps

Day	Training	Training Note
Monday	Easy 15 – 20 minute Jog.	Take walking breaks if necessary
Tuesday	Rest	
Wednesday	Easy 15 – 20 minute Jog.	Take walking breaks if necessary
Thursday	Rest	
Friday	Easy 20 minute jog	Take walking breaks if necessary
Saturday	Rest	
Sunday	25 minute walk / jog	Take it very easy

Day	PACES	MILES	TIME	ROUTE & NOTES
Mon				
Tue				
Wed				
Thurs				
Fri				
Sat				
Sun				

Note:

Week 2 Consolidate

Day	Training	Training Note
Monday	Rest	Recovery from Sunday's longer session.
Tuesday	20 minute jog	
Wednesday	Rest	
Thursday	20 – 25 minute jog	
Friday	Rest	
Saturday	Rest	
Sunday	25 minute walk / jog	

Day	PACES	MILES	TIME	ROUTE & NOTES
Mon				
Tue				
Wed				
Thurs				
Fri				
Sat				
Sun				

Note:

Week 3

Day	Training	Training Note
Monday	Rest	Recovery from Sunday's longer session.
Tuesday	25 minute jog	
Wednesday	Rest	
Thursday	30 minute jog	
Friday	Rest	
Saturday	Rest	
Sunday	35 minute non-stop run /jog	continuous Try and make it

Day	PACES	MILES	TIME	ROUTE & NOTES
Mon				
Tue				
Wed				
Thurs				
Fri				
Sat				
Sun				

Note:

Week 4 Moving up

Day	Training	Training Note
Monday	15 minute very easy	Leave the stopwatch recovery jog at home!
Tuesday	25 minute steady	
Wednesday	Rest	
Thursday	25 minute steady	
Friday	Rest	
Saturday	Rest	
Sunday	35 minute non-stop run /jog	Repeat of last Sunday, run / jog improve on time if possible

Day	PACES	MILES	TIME	ROUTE & NOTES
Mon				
Tue				
Wed				
Thurs				
Fri				
Sat				
Sun				

Note:

Week 5

Day	Training	Training Note
Monday	15 minute very easy recovery jog	Recovery session
Tuesday	Rest	
Wednesday	25 - 30 minute steady pace	
Thursday	Rest	
Friday	25 minute easy	
Saturday	Rest	
Sunday	40 – 45 minute jog/walk	Take walking breaks as necessary

Day	PACES	MILES	TIME	ROUTE & NOTES
Mon				
Tue				
Wed				
Thurs				
Fri				
Sat				
Sun				

Note:

Week 6

Day	Training	Training Note
Monday	20 minute easy recovery jog	Easy pace
Tuesday	25 – 30 minute steady	
Wednesday	Rest	
Thursday	35 minute steady	
Friday	Rest	
Saturday	Rest	
Sunday	40 – 45 minute	Try to jog / run non-stop

Day	PACES	MILES	TIME	ROUTE & NOTES
Mon				
Tue				
Wed				
Thurs				
Fri				
Sat				
Sun				

Note:

Week 7 First peak week

Day	Training	Training Note
Monday	20 minute recovery jog	Easy pace
Tuesday	25 – 30 minute steady	Big week, 5 runs
Wednesday	Rest	
Thursday	35 - 40 minute steady	
Friday	Rest	
Saturday	10 minute very easy jog	Only jogging
Sunday	1 hour slow	Don't push pace; take walking breaks if you feel like it.

Day	PACES	MILES	TIME	ROUTE & NOTES
Mon				
Tue				
Wed				
Thurs				
Fri				
Sat				
Sun				

Note:

Week 8 Taper week and lead-in 10 race

Day	Training	Training Note
Monday	Rest	
Tuesday	25 – 30 minute steady	
Wednesday	Rest	
Thursday	25 - 30 minute easy	
Friday	Rest	
Saturday	10 minute very easy jog	
Sunday	10k race + walking warm-up and cool-down	Take it easy

Day	PACES	MILES	TIME	ROUTE & NOTES
Mon				
Tue				
Wed				
Thurs				
Fri				
Sat				
Sun				

Note:

Schedule 2: Marathon training

Week 1 Building up

Day	Training	Training Note
Monday	25 minute jog	Just jogging very light
Tuesday	40 minute steady	
Wednesday	Rest	
Thursday	35 – 40 minute	
Friday	Rest	
Saturday	15 minute very easy	
Sunday	75 minute easy run	Take walking breaks if neede

Day	PACES	MILES	TIME	ROUTE & NOTES
Mon				
Tue				
Wed				
Thurs				
Fri				
Sat				
Sun				

Note:

Week 2

Day	Training	Training Note
Monday	Rest	
Tuesday	40 minute steady	
Wednesday	Rest	
Thursday	50 minute comfortable pace	
Friday	Rest	
Saturday	15 minute very easy	
Sunday	75 minute run	Repeat last Sunday's session with fewer walking breaks + warm-up and cool-down.

Day	PACES	MILES	TIME	ROUTE & NOTES
Mon				
Tue				
Wed				
Thurs				
Fri				
Sat				
Sun				

Note:

Week 3

Day	Training	Training Note
Monday	20 minute recovery jog	
Tuesday	40 minute steady	
Wednesday	Rest	
Thursday	50 minute	
Friday	Rest	
Saturday	Rest	
Sunday	80 – 90 minute jog with walking breaks	

Day	PACES	MILES	TIME	ROUTE & NOTES
Mon				
Tue				
Wed				
Thurs				
Fri				
Sat				
Sun				

Note:

Week 4

Day	Training	Training Note
Monday	20 minute recovery run	
Tuesday	40 minute steady pace	
Wednesday	Rest	
Thursday	Rest	Double rest before brisk run
Friday	40 minute brisk pace	
Saturday	Rest	
Sunday	90 – 100 minute slow	Very, very easy. Take a drink with you.

Day	PACES	MILES	TIME	ROUTE & NOTES
Mon				
Tue				
Wed				
Thurs				
Fri				
Sat				
Sun				

Note:

Week 5 Gradually building towards half marathon

Day	Training	Training Note
Monday	Rest	Day off after long effort
Tuesday	50 minute steady	
Wednesday	Rest	
Thursday	40 minute steady	
Friday	20 minute easy	
Saturday	Rest	
Sunday	100 – 110 minute easy	

Day	PACES	MILES	TIME	ROUTE & NOTES
Mon				
Tue				
Wed				
Thurs				
Fri				
Sat				
Sun				

Note:

Week 6

Day	Training	Training Note
Monday	Rest	
Tuesday	20 minute steady	
Wednesday	65 minute easy	
Thursday	Rest	
Friday	40 minute	
Saturday	Rest	
Sunday	120 minute taken very easy	Slow with drinks

Day	PACES	MILES	TIME	ROUTE & NOTES
Mon				
Tue				
Wed				
Thurs				
Fri				
Sat				
Sun				

Note:

Week 7 Taper week and half marathon race		
Day	Training	Training Note
Monday	Rest	
Tuesday	30 – 30 minute steady	
Wednesday	30 minute steady	
Thursday	Rest	
Friday	Rest	
Saturday	10 minute jog	Really slow, just to keep loose
Sunday	Half marathon (13.1 miles) + walk warm-up and cool-down	Slow all the way, just a training run

Day	PACES	MILES	TIME	ROUTE & NOTES
Mon				
Tue				
Wed				
Thurs				
Fri				
Sat				
Sun				

Note:

Week 8 Start of peak mileage phase		
Day	Training	Training Note
Monday	10 – 20 minute recovery session	Really slow
Tuesday	Rest	
Wednesday	30 minute steady	
Thursday	60 minute brisk	
Friday	Rest	
Saturday	30 minute jog	
Sunday	120 minute comfortable pace	

Day	PACES	MILES	TIME	ROUTE & NOTES
Mon				
Tue				
Wed				
Thurs				
Fri				
Sat				
Sun				

Note:

Week 9

Day	Training	Training Note
Monday	30 minute easy	
Tuesday	Rest	
Wednesday	60 minute brisk	Try to improve on last week's 60 minute distance
Thursday	Rest	
Friday	40 minute steady	
Saturday	Rest	
Sunday	130 – 140 minute taken very easy	Long, slow, run with drinks

Day	PACES	MILES	TIME	ROUTE & NOTES
Mon				
Tue				
Wed				
Thurs				
Fri				
Sat				
Sun				

Note:

Week 10

Day	Training	Training Note
Monday	Rest	Recovery after Sunday's log session.
Tuesday	40 minute steady	
Wednesday	Rest	
Thursday	75 minute comfortable pace	
Friday	20 minute jog	
Saturday	Rest	
Sunday	140 – 150 minute taken very easy	Long and slow

Day	PACES	MILES	TIME	ROUTE & NOTES
Mon				
Tue				
Wed				
Thurs				
Fri				
Sat				
Sun				

Note:

Week 11

Day	Training	Training Note
Monday	10 – 20 minute recovery jog	
Tuesday	40 minute steady	
Wednesday	Rest	
Thursday	75 minute	
Friday	Rest	
Saturday	30 minute easy pace	
Sunday	150 – 160 comfortable	

Day	PACES	MILES	TIME	ROUTE & NOTES
Mon				
Tue				
Wed				
Thurs				
Fri				
Sat				
Sun				

Note:

Week 12

Day	Training	Training Note
Monday	30 minute easy	
Tuesday	Rest	
Wednesday	50 minute fast	Home time-trial!
Thursday	Rest	
Friday	50 minute easy	Avoid the temptation to run at the pace of Wednesday's session
Saturday	Rest	
Sunday	180 minute slow	Start slowly, take drinks

Day	PACES	MILES	TIME	ROUTE & NOTES
Mon				
Tue				
Wed				
Thurs				
Fri				
Sat				
Sun				

Note:

Week 13 Peak week

Day	Training	Training Note
Monday	20 minute jog recovery	
Tuesday	40 minute brisk pace	
Wednesday	Rest	
Thursday	60 minute steady	
Friday	Rest	
Saturday	Rest	Prepare for last big run
Sunday	200 minute slow	Last long run be economical

Day	PACES	MILES	TIME	ROUTE & NOTES
Mon				
Tue				
Wed				
Thurs				
Fri				
Sat				
Sun				

Note:

Week 14 Start of race taper

Day	Training	Training Note
Monday	20 minute slow jog or rest if tired	
Tuesday	30 minute brisk	
Wednesday	Rest	
Thursday	50 minute steady	
Friday	Rest	
Saturday	Rest	
Sunday	120 minute steady	

Day	PACES	MILES	TIME	ROUTE & NOTES
Mon				
Tue				
Wed				
Thurs				
Fri				
Sat				
Sun				

Note:

Week 15 Further tapering

Day	Training	Training Note
Monday	20 minute easy	
Tuesday	Rest	
Wednesday	40 minute easy	
Thursday	Rest	
Friday	Rest	
Saturday	10 minute jog	
Sunday	70 minute easy in race kit and shoes	Slower than race pace

Day	PACES	MILES	TIME	ROUTE & NOTES
Mon				
Tue				
Wed				
Thurs				
Fri				
Sat				
Sun				

Note:

Week 16 Final taper and preparation week		
Day	Training	Training Note
Monday	30 minute jog	
Tuesday	Rest	
Wednesday	20 minute jog	
Thursday	Rest	
Friday	Rest	
Saturday	10 minute very, very easy jog	Keep it slow
Sunday	Go to Marathon!	THE RACE!

Day	PACES	MILES	TIME	ROUTE & NOTES
Mon				
Tue				
Wed				
Thurs				
Fri				
Sat				
Sun				

Note:

Made in the USA
Las Vegas, NV
09 May 2024